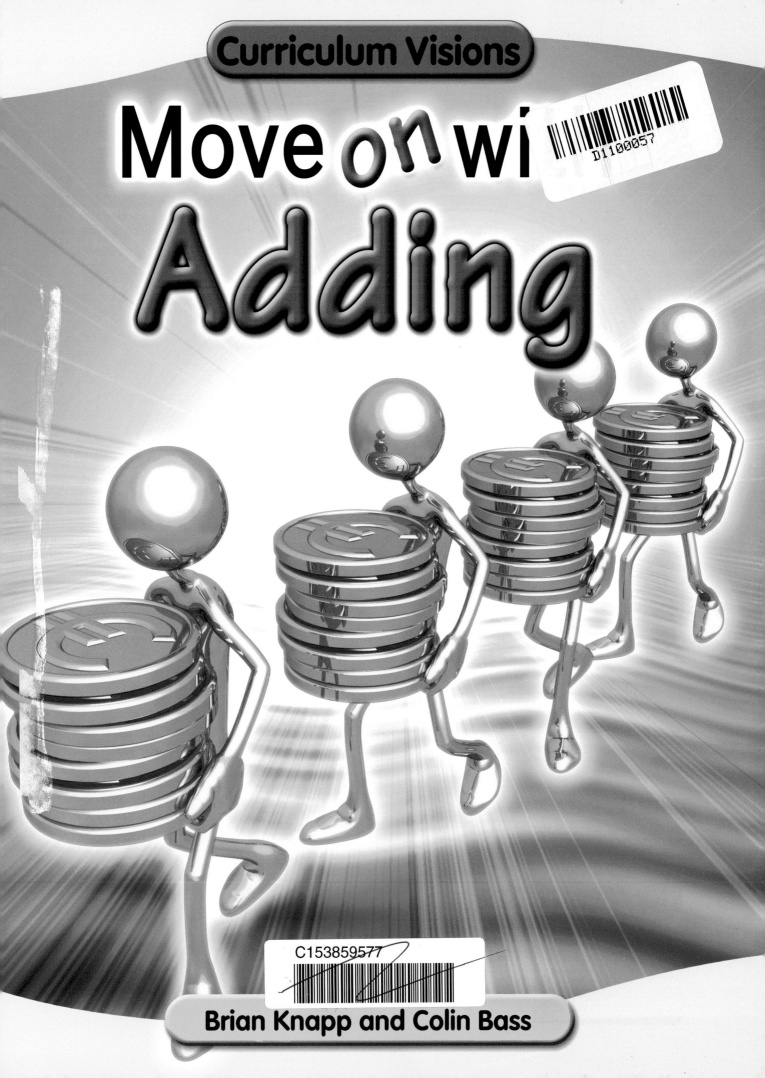

Curriculum Visions

Move on wi Adding

D1100057

C153859577

Brian Knapp and Colin Bass

Curriculum Visions

There's much more online including videos

You will find multimedia resources covering a wide range of topics at:

www.CurriculumVisions.com

CurriculumVisions is a subscription web site.

A CVP Book
Copyright © 2009 Atlantic Europe Publishing

Series Concept
Brian Knapp, BSc, PhD

Text contributed by
Brian Knapp, BSc, PhD,
and Colin Bass, BSc, MA

Editors
Lorna Gilbert, Barbara Carragher,
and Gillian Gatehouse

Senior Designer
Adele Humphries, BA, PGCE

Illustrations
David Woodroffe

Designed and produced by
Atlantic Europe Publishing

Printed in China by
WKT Company Ltd

Curriculum Visions Move on with Maths – Adding
A CIP record for this book is available from the British Library

ISBN: 978 1 86214 555 9

Picture credits
All photographs are from the Earthscape Picture Library and ShutterStock collections.

This product is manufactured from sustainable managed forests. For every tree cut down at least one more is planted.

Move on with Maths Resources CD

You will find hundreds of photocopiable word problems in the teacher's 'Move on with Maths Resources CD', which is available for separate purchase.

Look out for these sections to help you learn more about each topic:

 Remember... This provides a summary of the key concept(s) on each two-page entry. Use it to revise what you have learned.

Can you do this? These problems reinforce the concepts learned on a particular spread, and can be used to test existing knowledge.

Answers to the problems set in the 'Move on with Maths' series can be found at: **www.curriculumvisions.com/moveOnAnswers**

Place value

To make it easy for you to see exactly what we are doing, you will find coloured columns behind the numbers in all the examples on this and the following pages. This is what the colours mean:

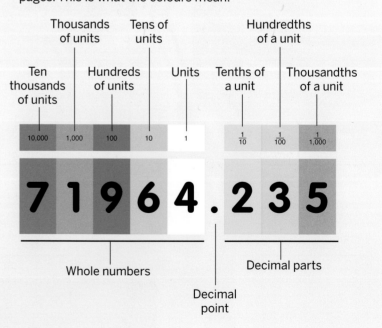

Ten thousands of units — 10,000
Thousands of units — 1,000
Hundreds of units — 100
Tens of units — 10
Units — 1
Tenths of a unit — $\frac{1}{10}$
Hundredths of a unit — $\frac{1}{100}$
Thousandths of a unit — $\frac{1}{1,000}$

7 1 9 6 4 . 2 3 5

Whole numbers

Decimal parts

Decimal point

Contents

4   Counting on

6   Using a ruler to add

8   Using two rulers to add

10   Adding using patterns

12   First adding facts

14   Using columns to add

16   Add in any order

18   Beginning an adding square

20   Adding facts for 10 or more

22   The complete adding square

24   Adding from 10 to 99

26   Adding several numbers

28   Adding bigger numbers

30   Decimal numbers

32   Adding minus numbers

34   Adding fractions

36   Adding to an equation

38   Distance charts

40   What symbols mean

40   Index

Counting on

Counting is the simplest thing you can do with numbers. It is just a matter of moving on one number at a time.

A good example of how to count on is the way we use our fingers and calendars. In a calendar all the dates for each month are shown. We use counting on to find out such things as how long it is to the next basketball match, or how long it is to a friend's birthday.

How many days?

Emily's mother told her that Aunt Emma's birthday would be in five days' time. Emily wanted to know what date that would be. She knew that today was September **16th**. So she needed to count on from then. Emily used her fingers to help her count on from the **16th**:

1 In one day it would be the **17th**.

2 In two days it would be the **18th**.

3 In three days it would be the **19th**.

4 In four days it would be the **20th**.

5 And in five days it would be the **21st**.

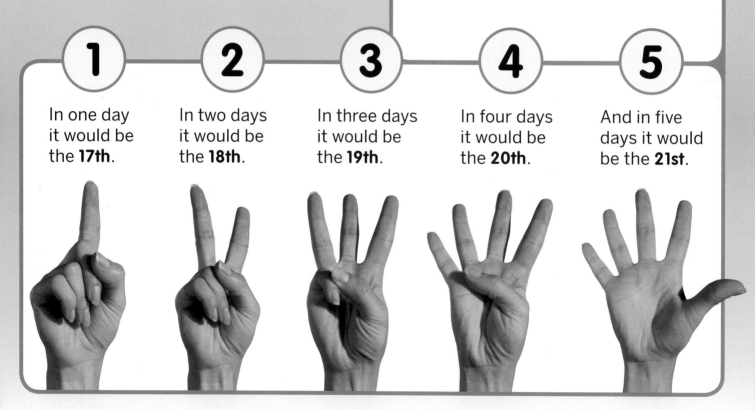

 Remember… In counting you work through the numbers one (or two etc) at a time. You can count up or down.

Speed up: count in twos!

People who use counting a lot often count two at a time. If you worked in a warehouse you might have to count up the number of items on the shelves. You would soon get fed up counting one at a time. Interestingly, counting in twos (**2, 4, 6, 8…**) not only cuts the counting time in half, but people lose their place less easily!

Try counting these sweets in pairs to see that it is faster. Start from the front. Notice that the sweets are not arranged regularly towards the back, so it's harder to count and this breaks your speed. Arranging things helps further, as we will see on page 12.

Counting long numbers

Counting on with your fingers is easy when the number involved is **10** or less. But Emily also knew that it would be her brother's birthday in **23** days' time and she wanted to find out what the date would be. So was there an easier way to find out than using fingers?

Emily could certainly have used another method that didn't need fingers if she'd had a calendar handy. She could have counted on using the dates printed on the calendar.

By counting on using the calendar, you can see that her brother's birthday is on Thursday, **9th** October.

SEPTEMBER

SUN	MON	TUE	WED	THU	FRI	SAT
	1	2	3	4	5	6
7	8	9	10	11	12	13
14	15	⓰ →	17 →	18 →	19 →	20 →
21 →	22 →	23 →	24 →	25 →	26 →	27 →
28 →	29 →	30 →				

OCTOBER

SUN	MON	TUE	WED	THU	FRI	SAT
			1 →	2 →	3 →	4 →
5 →	6 →	7 →	8 →	⑨	10	11
12	13	14	15	16	17	18
19	20	21	22	23	24	25
26	27	28	29	30		

Can you do this? Use the calendar to find out how many days it is from the **15th** to the **26th**.

Using a ruler to add

A ruler is a simple number line which we can use to count with.

The idea of counting on is at the heart of adding. When we are adding, we are always asking, "What is the answer when we add (count on) one number to another?" To make this easy, we can use a simple number line, such as the ruler marked off in whole numbers shown below.

Jackie has a collection of **4** books. She buys (adds) **5** more. How many has she got now?

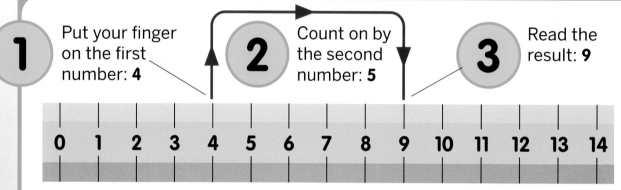

1 Put your finger on the first number: **4**

2 Count on by the second number: **5**

3 Read the result: **9**

A ruler used as a number line for counting.

One way of showing what we have done is to use words, for example:

Four plus five equals nine

Or as a word equation:

Four and five makes nine

And as a number equation this is:

$$4 + 5 = 9$$

Remember... To add using a ruler, put your finger on the first number, count along the ruler by the second number and read off the result.

Counting on waiting

Frank phoned up his local record shop to find out how long he would have to wait for the new CD going on sale that day. He was told about **23** minutes. When he arrived at the shop, he found that lots more people had recently joined the queue, and the wait had gone up by **8** minutes more than he was told on the phone. How long would Frank have to wait?

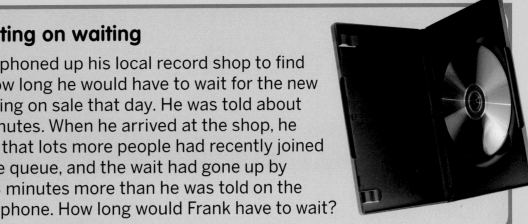

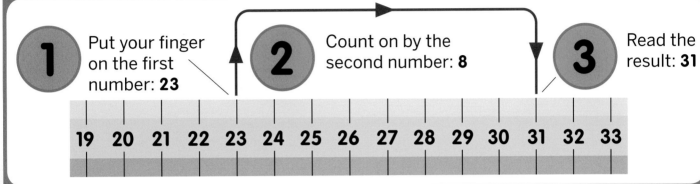

1 Put your finger on the first number: **23**

2 Count on by the second number: **8**

3 Read the result: **31**

| 19 | 20 | 21 | 22 | 23 | 24 | 25 | 26 | 27 | 28 | 29 | 30 | 31 | 32 | 33 |

So, Frank had to wait for **31** minutes. We can write what we have done as:

Twenty three plus eight makes thirty one

Which as a number equation is: **23 + 8 = 31**

Adding up your savings

Emily had **£19** in her piggy bank. Her Gran gave her **£15** for her birthday, and Emily decided to spend **£10** and save the other **£5**. How much does she have saved now?

Method

Find **19** on the ruler. (This is what she had already saved.) Count on **5** more marks. (This is what she is saving.) You should reach **24**. We can write this as:

Nineteen and five makes twenty four

which as a number equation is:

19 + 5 = 24

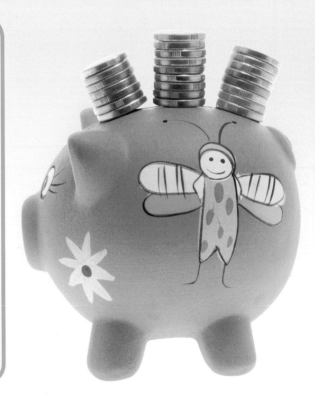

Can you do this? Use the ruler to count **13** on from **20**.

Using two rulers to add

Two rulers show you the basics of adding.

To speed up your counting, you can use two rulers side by side. This will make an adding slide rule to help you with simple adding problems.

Problem

To add **3** and **9** by sliding rulers.   **3 + 9 = ?**

1 Put the zero of ruler B against the first number to be added on ruler A. In this case it is **3**.

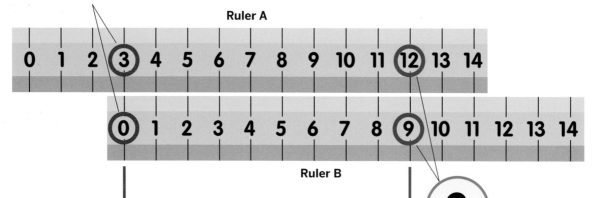

Ruler A

Ruler B

2 Look along ruler B until you come to the second number to be added. In this case it is **9**.

3 Read the answer off ruler A opposite the second number. In this case it is **12**.

From the rulers we can therefore work out that: **3 + 9 = 12**

>>> **Remember...** To add with two rulers, you place the zero of one ruler against the first number you want to add on the other ruler. Then look along the second ruler until you find the next number. Read the answer off the first ruler.

Problem

To add **12** and **15** using two rulers. **12 + 15 = ?**

1 Put the zero of ruler B against the first number to be added on ruler A. In this case it is **12**.

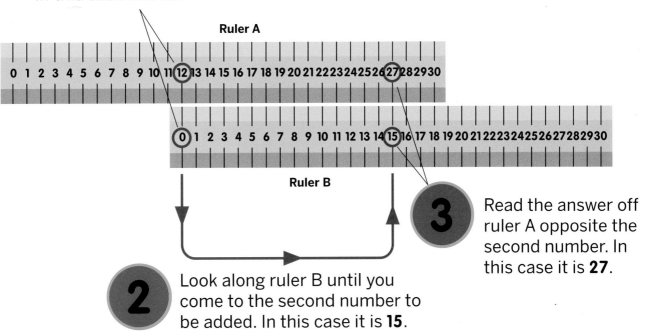

Ruler A

Ruler B

2 Look along ruler B until you come to the second number to be added. In this case it is **15**.

3 Read the answer off ruler A opposite the second number. In this case it is **27**.

Therefore the sum of twelve and fifteen is twenty seven: **12 + 15 = 27**

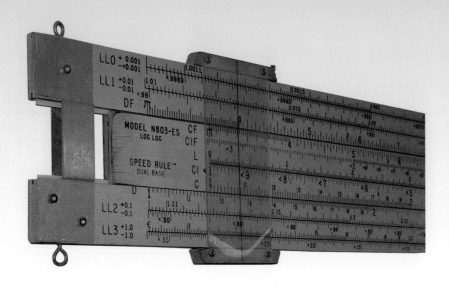

Until the invention of electronic calculators, double and triple rulers were used by engineers and scientists to do many kinds of calculations. These ruler sets were called slide rules.

Can you do this? Use the rulers to add **8** and **17**.

Work the answer out on a separate piece of paper.

Adding using patterns

We find it very slow and difficult to count large quantities of things. Arranging them in patterns can make it easier for us to add them.

Let's look at an example. The nest on the right contains eggs. But can you see how many of them there are at a glance?

You probably found this difficult, because most of us find it difficult to recognise a group of more than five objects at a glance. After that the brain needs some help, and we have to start counting!

The importance of patterns

Just think about the way you worked out how many eggs there were in the picture above. You had to count the eggs one at a time. Now look at the eggs in the box on the right.

Did you count every egg to find out how many there were?

Or did you count along one row to get **6** and then say to yourself:

"There are two rows of **6**, and so there are **12** eggs in the box"?

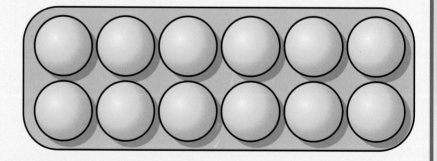

Your brain added two counting numbers together. We would say this as:

6 eggs and 6 eggs makes 12 eggs

And using symbols, it is:

6 + 6 = 12

Working fast with patterns

Your brain works faster with patterns. This is the reason playing cards have their markings arranged in patterns.

Notice that by using patterns, you can easily recognise a card with a value of **8**, **9** or **10**:

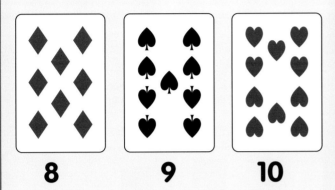

8   **9**   **10**

But how did your brain do this? Well, it probably looked at the patterns, counted the marks in one pattern, noticed there was more than one similar pattern, and **put together, or added**, the number in each pattern.

For example, a 'ten' card has **2** patterns of **5** marks. You might say to yourself, "**5** and **5** hearts makes **10** hearts".

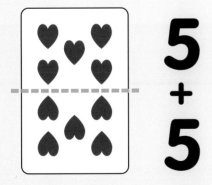

$$5 + 5$$

Using symbols, it is:

$$5 + 5 = 10$$

Practise adding and check

When you throw dice, you do not know which face will fall upwards.

Remember to work with the patterns, but if you have trouble, just count the dots to check your answer.

Group 1

Group 2

 Remember… Thinking in terms of patterns can speed up your work. Easy patterns include **2's**, **5's** and **10's**.

Can you do this? Throw dice for yourself and practise adding them as fast as you can.

First adding facts

Many simple additions can be held in your head. These then become adding facts.

How can you easily count a total of eight pieces of chocolate? To find out, you can arrange them into groups. At the same time, you will produce a collection of important adding facts.

This is the shape used for a single chocolate piece. It can also be called a **unit**.

1 These are the chocolate pieces laid out with no pattern.

2 The same set of pieces has now been put into a line.

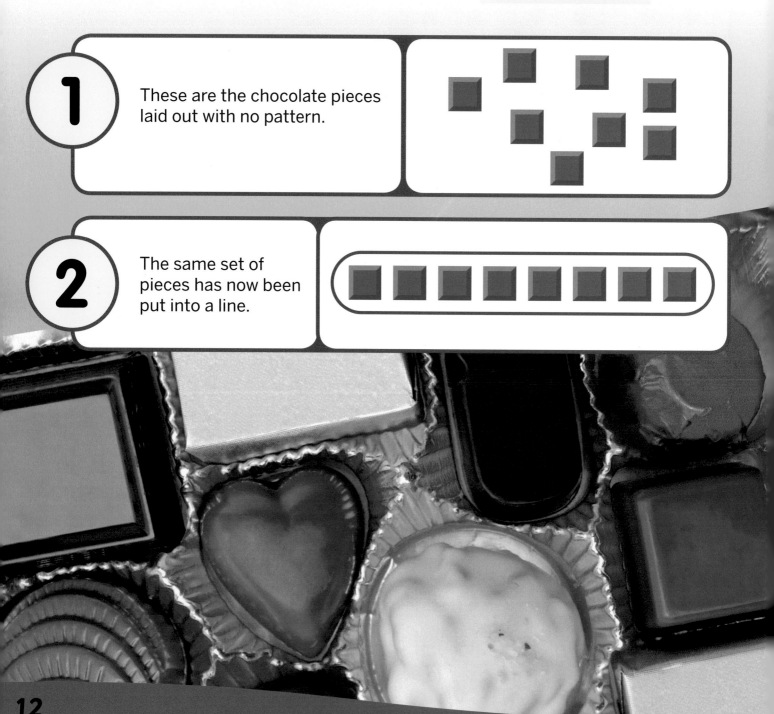

12

3 The pieces have now been arranged into groups. The numbers tell you how many are in each group. There are always eight pieces in each line in this example:

Line 1   1 + 7 = 8

Line 2   2 + 6 = 8

Line 3   3 + 5 = 8

Line 4   4 + 4 = 8

Notice that we have shown the mathematical symbols above each line.

1 + 7 = 8   **2 + 6 = 8**   **3 + 5 = 8**   **4 + 4 = 8**

Suppose you have eaten one of the chocolates, and seven are left. (Don't eat any more just now.) You can arrange them to show that

1 + 6 = 7

2 + 5 = 7

3 + 4 = 7

Can you do this? Suppose you had started out yesterday with nine chocolates. On a separate piece of paper, list the adding facts you can find.

Using columns to add

Numbers are most easily added by placing them in columns.

It is always best to try to find simple, easily understood ways of writing things down. Here is how we write down a sum of two single numbers, also called single digits.

First, we have to plan ahead. Later in the book we will be adding together some very big numbers. But putting large numbers in rows makes adding very difficult. So we put them in columns instead.

The key idea is to make sure the numbers are exactly one above the other in the columns. We will guide you in this book by using coloured columns. In this case the yellow colour of the column also tells you that the numbers are all units (see page 2 for more help with coloured columns).

For example, we can put **3 + 4 = 7** into columns like this:

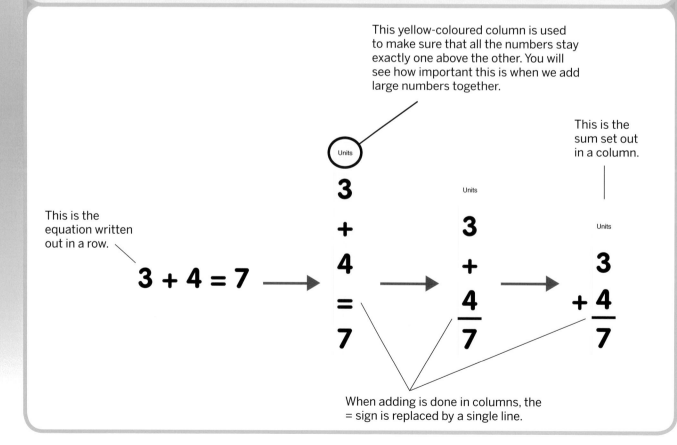

This yellow-coloured column is used to make sure that all the numbers stay exactly one above the other. You will see how important this is when we add large numbers together.

This is the sum set out in a column.

This is the equation written out in a row.

$$3 + 4 = 7$$

Units

3
+
4
=
7

Units

3
+
4
7

Units

3
+ 4
7

When adding is done in columns, the = sign is replaced by a single line.

Here are three more simple examples to help you to see how adding columns works.

$$4 + 5 = 9 \longrightarrow \begin{array}{c} 4 \\ + \\ 5 \\ = \\ 9 \end{array} \longrightarrow \begin{array}{r} 4 \\ + 5 \\ \hline 9 \end{array}$$

$$2 + 5 = 7 \longrightarrow \begin{array}{c} 2 \\ + \\ 5 \\ = \\ 7 \end{array} \longrightarrow \begin{array}{r} 2 \\ + 5 \\ \hline 7 \end{array}$$

$$2 + 7 = 9 \longrightarrow \begin{array}{c} 2 \\ + \\ 7 \\ = \\ 9 \end{array} \longrightarrow \begin{array}{r} 2 \\ + 7 \\ \hline 9 \end{array}$$

>>> **Remember...** You place numbers in columns for adding. You don't have to draw in the columns, but you should always write out your work in columns.

Can you do these? On a separate piece of paper, can you rearrange these into columns:

3 + 5 = 8

6 + 2 = 8

Add in any order

We can take a group of things and separate them in different ways, but the total number of things remains the same, no matter how we split them up.

For example, if we take a group of seven things, we can split them into different groups like this. They always add up to **7**.

Line 1   1 + 6 = 7

Line 2   2 + 5 = 7

Line 3   3 + 4 = 7

Line 4   4 + 3 = 7

Line 5   5 + 2 = 7

Line 6   6 + 1 = 7

Here you can also see one of the important facts to learn about adding: whatever order the numbers are added in, they still make the same total.

This means that it doesn't matter which order you add, the total will always be the same. This is called the 'Turn-Around Rule': you can turn the numbers around as much as you want in adding, the sum will always be the same.

For example, in line 1 on the opposite page you have a group of **1** and a group of **6**.

$$1 + 6 = 7$$

On line 6 you will see that the things have been arranged so that there is a group of **6** and a group of **1**. But the total is still **7**.

$$6 + 1 = 7$$

You will find the same patterns in each of the other combinations of groups in the pattern.

Lines 3 and 4

$$3 + 4 = 7 \text{ and } 4 + 3 = 7$$

Lines 2 and 5

$$2 + 5 = 7 \text{ and } 5 + 2 = 7$$

 Remember... Adding follows the 'Turn-Around Rule'. When we add the same two numbers, the answer is the same no matter which of the numbers comes first.

Looking at the chocolates below you can see that:

$$1 + 7 = 8$$
and
$$7 + 1 = 8$$
Also
$$2 + 6 = 8$$
and
$$6 + 2 = 8$$
And
$$3 + 5 = 8$$
and
$$5 + 3 = 8$$

Use your calculator...
The fact that numbers can be added in any order remains true for huge numbers as well.
So, **98,047 + 537,165 = 635,212** and **537,165 + 98,047 = 635,212**. Check this using your calculator.

Can you do this? Try adding in different orders with the adding facts you found out when there were nine chocolates ('Can you do this?', page 13).

Give your working out on a separate piece of paper.

Beginning an adding square

Adding squares put adding facts into patterns that are easy to see.

Adding saves time compared with counting. First, we don't have to go back to the beginning every time. Second, we can learn some simple sums which are always the same, and which we can use over and over again. These are called adding facts. Adding facts can be placed together in a square to make learning them easier.

Adding facts to 9

It is very important to learn adding facts if we are to do adding well. There are three steps:

1 Check that the facts we are using are correct.

2 Find a neat way of writing down the facts, so that we don't have to keep checking them.

3 Learn them by heart.

We found out some adding facts on earlier pages. On the right you can see a neat way to write down these adding facts and many others besides.

We first write down each of the numbers between **0** and **9** to make two of the sides of our square.

Then we fill in the sums as you can see on the next page.

+	0	1	2	3	4	5	6	7	8	9
0										
1										
2										
3										
4										
5										
6										
7										
8										
9										

How to use the adding square

1 You choose the first number you want to add from the top row.

2 You choose the other number you want to add from the left column.

Follow along the row from the second number.

3 You read the answer from where the row and column cross.

Follow down the column from the first number, **5**.

Read the answer to the adding sum.

+	0	1	2	3	4	5	6	7	8	9
0	0	1	2	3	4	5	6	7	8	9
1	1	2	3	4	5	6	7	8	9	
2	2	3	4	5	6	7	8	9		
3	3	4	5	6	7	8	9			
4	4	5	6	7	8	9				
5	5	6	7	8	9					
6	6	7	8	9						
7	7	8	9							
8	8	9								
9	9									

See the adding square completed on page 23.

Example: To add **5** and **3** using the adding square, follow down from the **5** in the top row and along from **3** in the left column to get to **8** in the square.

5 + 3 = 8

or follow across from **5** in the left column and down from **3** in the top row.

 Remember... An adding square makes it easier to learn the sum of two small numbers. These are the numbers we use every day.

Can you do these? Use the adding square above to find **2 + 4** and **3 + 6**.

Adding facts for 10 or more

To get larger adding facts we need to count in columns and carry to the left.

Sometimes, when we count up two single-digit numbers (units), such as **4 + 7**, the total comes to **10** or more. But we can only put up to **9** in any one column. If we want to put down more than **9**, we have to carry over the extra amount to the next column on the left. Here is the method for adding these kinds of numbers.

Begin by counting these oranges:

　　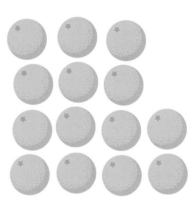

nine	**and**	**five**	**count up to** **fourteen**

We can write this as an equation by replacing words with symbols: **9 + 5 = 14**

Similarly:

ten	**and** **four equals**	**fourteen**

Which we can write as: **10 + 4 = 14**

Using columns

The columns hold our numbers. We are using coloured columns to remind us that where we place a number is very important.

When we place it on the right (in a yellow-coloured column), we are saying its value is only units (**1** to **9**).

When we place it in the next column to the left (a gold-coloured column), we are saying that its value is in the tens (**10** to **90**).

If there are no units, we hold the place of the units open by putting a **0** in the yellow column.

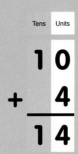

There is a **1** (one ten) in the tens column and **0** (zero) in the units column. We are adding **4** units, so we put the **4** below the **0**. The result is **0 + 4 = 4** in the units column and **1(+ 0)** in the tens column, giving the answer **14**.

Carrying to the left

We use the same idea for adding **9 + 5** as we did for **10 + 4**.

Both **9** and **5** are units, so they go above one another in the units column.

We know from the opposite page that **9 + 5 = 10 + 4**, so we put **4** in the units column and carry **1** into the tens column where we write it down.

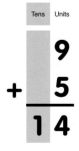

These numbers come to more than **9**. Put one of the **5** units with the **9** to make **10**, carry it into the next column. Four units are left from the five, and these are written down in the units column.

Remember... We cannot put more than **9** in a column; we have to carry over the extra amount to the next column on the left.

Can you do this? 5 + 7 = ?

Work the answer out on a separate piece of paper.

The complete adding square

Here is an adding square for numbers up to 9

The number facts above **9** that we began to see on page 21 can easily be included in the adding square. They all have a single **1** in the tens column. No number in the square is greater than **18** because **9 + 9 = 18**.

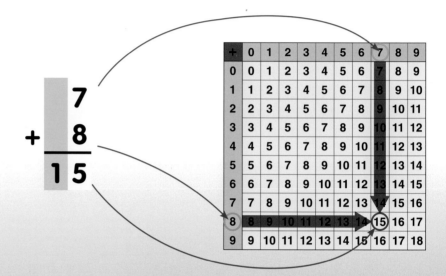

Enough sausages?

Fred went to the freezer to get some sausages. His mum wanted at least **16** for their family supper. Fred found that one bag of loose sausages contained **9** sausages, while another contained **8**. He took a small copy of the adding table out of his shirt pocket and read the answer. It was **17**, and so he was able to leave one sausage in the freezer and take out the rest (**16 + 1 = 17**).

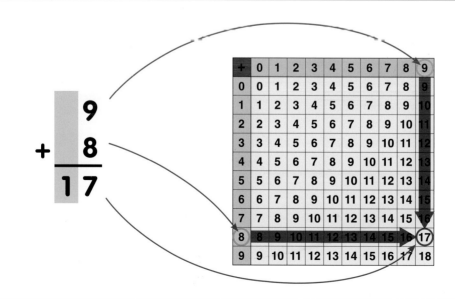

Here is a large copy of the adding square so that you can practise looking up more adding facts.

+	0	1	2	3	4	5	6	7	8	9
0	0	1	2	3	4	5	6	7	8	9
1	1	2	3	4	5	6	7	8	9	10
2	2	3	4	5	6	7	8	9	10	11
3	3	4	5	6	7	8	9	10	11	12
4	4	5	6	7	8	9	10	11	12	13
5	5	6	7	8	9	10	11	12	13	14
6	6	7	8	9	10	11	12	13	14	15
7	7	8	9	10	11	12	13	14	15	16
8	8	9	10	11	12	13	14	15	16	17
9	9	10	11	12	13	14	15	16	17	18

 Remember... To look for patterns. If you can find patterns in the mathematics you learn, you will find many easy ways to learn facts, and also many short cuts. In this case you will know that although there are **100** adding facts in the square, because numbers can be added in any order, you only have to learn half of them.

For adding in columns you do not need the square to go beyond **9**. But you can make and learn your own squares. Here is one that works in **6's**.

0	6	12	18	24	30
6	12	18	24	30	36
12	18	24	30	36	42
18	24	30	36	42	48
24	30	36	42	48	54
30	36	42	48	54	60

Can you do these? Use the adding square above to find **9 + 8** and **7 + 9**.

Adding from 10 to 99

This is simple when you use columns to add and carry left.

We have already used columns to help with our adding. On this page you can really see how useful this is. All the numbers on this page contain two-digit numbers (that is, numbers between **10** and **99**), so there is always a number in the tens column as well as a number in the units column. In the last of the examples, the answer is in the hundreds. This is a three-digit number that uses three columns.

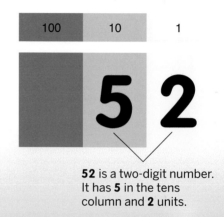

52 is a two-digit number. It has **5** in the tens column and **2** units.

Here is how to add two two-digit numbers. In this example the answer is also two digits: **52 + 26 = ?**

1 Line up the numbers. Put one number below the other in a column, lining the numbers up on the right. Draw a line below them. The answer goes below the line.

$$52$$
$$+ 26$$
$$? ?$$

> Numbers to add
—— Answer goes here

2 Start with units. Add the right-hand column first. In this case **2 + 6 = 8**.

$$52$$
$$+ 26$$
$$? 8$$

> 2 + 6 = 8

3 Now add the next column to the left. This is the tens column: **5 + 2 = 7**. (Really **50 + 20 = 70**)

5 + 2 = 7

$$52$$
$$+ 26$$
$$7 8$$

—— Answer, **78** (**7** tens, **8** units)

Remember... Each column has a value: units, tens, hundreds. If adding a column gives an answer bigger than **9**, you carry the left-hand number to the next column to the left, writing it down below that column so you don't forget it.

In this example the answer is a three-digit number: **92 + 46 = ?**

1 Line up the numbers. Put one number below the other in a column, lining the numbers up on the right.

```
    9 2
+   4 6
  ? ? ?
```

2 Add the right-hand column first: **2 + 6 = 8**.

```
    9 2
+   4 6
  ? ? 8
```

These numbers in the units column add to less than **10**, and so there is nothing to carry over.

3 Now add tens. Add the next column to the left. This is the tens column. We are actually adding up tens: so **9 + 4 (= 13)** is really **90 + 40 = 130**. Write down **3**, carry **1**.

```
    9 2
+   4 6
  ? 3 8
  1
```

The number carried over is really ten **10's** (which we write as **100**), so now the carried **1** goes into the hundreds column.

4 There are no more columns of numbers to add above the line to the left, so the number carried over is placed, on its own, in the hundreds column.
   This makes the final answer **138**.

```
    9 2
+   4 6
  1 3 8
```

This is the carried-over number.

Here are some more examples for you to look at.

```
    3 9          5 1          6 4          6 7
+   7 0      +   5 2      +   7 5      +   8 1
  1 0 9        1 0 3        1 3 9        1 4 8
    1            1            1            1
```

Can you do these?

Work the answers out on a separate piece of paper.

```
    8 7          8 3          7 4          9 1
+   4 2      +   8 3      +   8 3      +   9 8
  ? ? ?        ? ? ?        ? ? ?        ? ? ?
```

Adding several numbers

In many cases you have to add several numbers together.

Take these numbers, for example: **13 + 35 + 46 + 57 = ?**

 **1**

They are the numbers of coupons collected by each member of a club. The club leader needed to know the total because when the club had enough coupons, the local superstore would give them a new computer.

The club leader lined the numbers up in a long column to add them together.

	100	10	1
		1	3
		3	5
		4	6
+		5	7

 2

First add the units column.

To do this, either add from the top or the bottom. In this case we add from the top down.

We add the top two numbers in the right-hand column first:

3 + 5 = 8

Now add the next number to this total:

8 + 6 = 14

Now add the last number to this total:

14 + 7 = 21

Write **1** in the units column, carry **2** into the tens column.

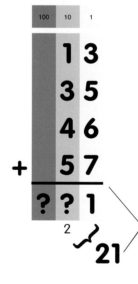

The numbers in the units column add up to **21**. The **1** unit is written in the units column, and the **2** representing **2** tens, or **20**, is written below the tens column.

>>>> **Remember...** The longer the column of figures, the easier it is to make a mistake. So it is important to check the calculation. We do this by adding in the opposite order. In this way we add different numbers together and are less likely to repeat any mistake we might have made the first time.

3

Next add the tens column.
   To do this, either add from the top or the bottom. In this case we have decided to add from the bottom upwards but you could, if you find it easier, add from the top.
We add the bottom number to the number carried over:

(2) + 5 = 7

Now add the next number to this total:

7 + 4 = 11

Now add the next number to this total:

11 + 3 = 14

Now add the top number to this total:

14 + 1 = 15

Write **5** in the tens column, carry **1** into the hundreds column.

Since there are no more hundreds to add, put **1** into the answer, which is **151**.

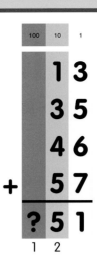

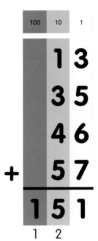

You can add the numbers in a column from top to bottom <u>or</u> bottom to top. See the Turn-Around Rule on page 17.

Here are some more examples for you to look at.

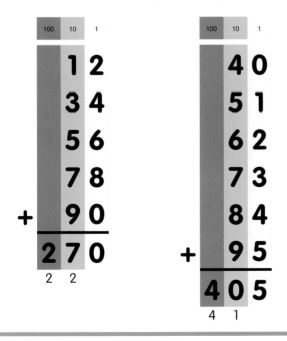

Use your calculator...
Electronic calculators are everywhere today. You should always work out single and two-digit additions in your head using the techniques shown in this book where possible. But for longer additions you may find a calculator useful.

Can you do this? Add **94, 34, 85, 21, 67, 85.**
Work the answer out on a separate piece of paper.

Adding bigger numbers

Very big numbers are just added using more columns.

A very big number, such as **645**, is six hundred (**600**) and (+) forty (**40**) (+) five (**5**). So it has three columns.

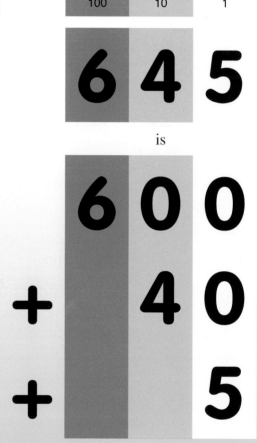

Charity raffle

The school had been planning a raffle to raise money for their favourite charities. They decided that there would be a competition between classes – everyone in the class that sold the most tickets would get a free burger lunch.

At the time of the raffle one class had sold **252** tickets, another class had sold **237** tickets, the third class had sold **216** tickets, but the fourth class had sold as many as **328** tickets.

While the winning class set off to get its free lunch, the head teacher found out how many tickets were actually sold.

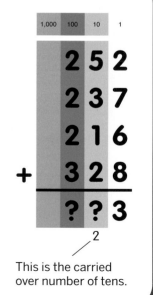

Line up the numbers, then start with the units.

In this case it is: **8 + 6 + 7 + 2 = 23**, that is **20 + 3**, so write down **3** in the units and carry **2** into the tens column.

This is the carried over number of tens.

2

Now add the tens column. Start with the carried over number:

(2)+ 2 + 1 + 3 + 5 = 13.
Since we are adding tens, this is really **130**.
Write down **3**, carry **1**.

1,000	100	10	1

```
    2 5 2
    2 3 7
    2 1 6
  + 3 2 8
  ---------
  ? ? 3 3
      1
```

This is the carried over number of hundreds.

3

Add the hundreds column. Start with the carried over number:

(1) + 3 + 2 + 2 + 2 (=10).
Since we are adding hundreds, this is really **1,000**.
    Write down **0** and carry **1**.
Since we have no more columns to the left we put the **1** in the thousands column.

```
    2 5 2
    2 3 7
    2 1 6
  + 3 2 8
  ---------
  1 0 3 3
  1
```

This is the carried over number of thousands.

≫≫≫ **Remember…** If you have to add big numbers, you will need more columns to work in. In this example we needed to draw in a thousands column.

Here are some more to look at.

```
    1 0 6
    1 3 8
    1 5 1
  + 6 4 5
  ---------
  1 0 4 0
    1 1 2
```

```
    1 2 3
    3 2 1
    4 5 6
  + 6 5 4
  ---------
  1 5 5 4
    1 1 1
```

```
    2 8 6
    1 1 6
    1 5 6
  + 9 9 9
  ---------
  1 5 5 7
    1 2 2
```

```
    1 1 1
    2 2 2
    3 3 3
  + 4 4 4
  ---------
  1 1 1 0
    1 1 1
```

Can you do this? Add **235, 524, 439, 265.**

Work the answer out on a separate piece of paper.

Decimal numbers

Decimals combine whole numbers with parts of numbers. But you still add them in columns.

Decimals are numbers that combine whole numbers with parts of whole numbers, for example, **2.31**.

To separate numbers with a value of **1** or more from numbers less than **1**, a mathematical 'full stop' is placed after the units so that we know which one it is. The full stop is called a decimal point.

Just as with whole numbers, which have the smallest part of the number on the right and the largest on the left, so every number to the right of the decimal point has a value ten times smaller than its left-hand neighbour. The further it is to the right, the smaller the number is. Numbers smaller than units are described as tenths, hundredths, thousandths, and so on, but are said differently, so that **0.67** is said 'nought-point-six-seven'.

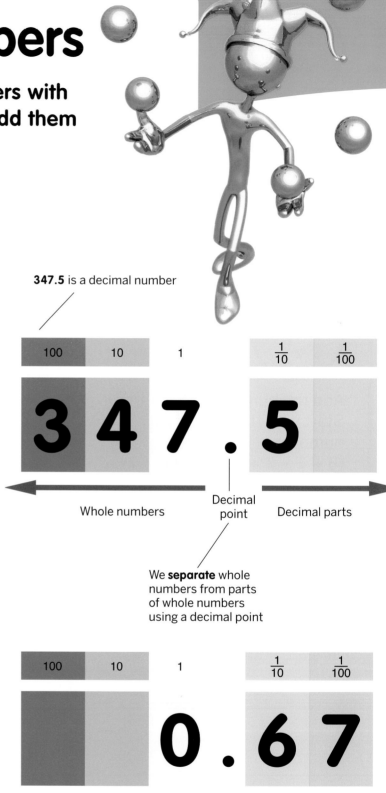

347.5 is a decimal number

| 100 | 10 | 1 | $\frac{1}{10}$ | $\frac{1}{100}$ |

3 4 7 . 5

Whole numbers   Decimal point   Decimal parts

We **separate** whole numbers from parts of whole numbers using a decimal point

| 100 | 10 | 1 | $\frac{1}{10}$ | $\frac{1}{100}$ |

0 . 6 7

 Remember... When adding decimal numbers, keep the decimal points in a column. Then add the decimal numbers just as you would add whole numbers, beginning on the right. At the end put a decimal point in the answer in line with the others.

Example: Add **347.5** and **26.67**

1 Place the numbers above each other, keeping the decimal points in a column.

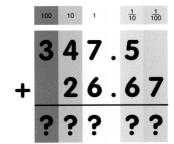

$$
\begin{array}{r}
3\,4\,7\,.\,5 \\
+\quad 2\,6\,.\,6\,7 \\
\hline
?\,?\,?\ ?\,?
\end{array}
$$

2 If the numbers have an unequal number of decimals, write extra zeros to fill the columns. In this case, a zero (**0**) has been written after the **347.5** to make it **347.50**.

$$
\begin{array}{r}
3\,4\,7\,.\,5\,0 \\
+\quad 2\,6\,.\,6\,7 \\
\hline
?\,?\,?\ ?\,?
\end{array}
$$

Write an extra **0** here

3 Start adding from the right as usual.

$$
\begin{array}{r}
3\,4\,7\,.\,5\,0 \\
+\quad 2\,6\,.\,6\,7 \\
\hline
3\,7\,4\ \ 1\,7
\end{array}
$$

4 Put a decimal point in the answer exactly below the other decimal points. This gives the final answer.

$$
\begin{array}{r}
3\,4\,7\,.\,5\,0 \\
+\quad 2\,6\,.\,6\,7 \\
\hline
3\,7\,4\,.\,1\,7
\end{array}
$$

The decimal numbers lined up

Here are some more examples for you to check:

$$
\begin{array}{r}
3\,1\,4\,.\,1\,6 \\
+\quad 3\,1\,.\,4\,2 \\
\hline
3\,4\,5\,.\,5\,8
\end{array}
$$

$$
\begin{array}{r}
5\,4\,3\,.\,2\,1 \\
+\quad 6\,7\,.\,8\,9 \\
\hline
6\,1\,1\,.\,1\,0
\end{array}
$$

$$
\begin{array}{r}
1\,7\,9\,.\,6\,7 \\
+\,1\,7\,9\,.\,3\,3 \\
\hline
3\,5\,9\,.\,0\,0
\end{array}
$$

$$
\begin{array}{r}
2\,5\,9\,.\,1\,6 \\
+\,3\,8\,2\,.\,7\,1 \\
\hline
6\,4\,1\,.\,8\,7
\end{array}
$$

Can you do these?
Add **23.7** and **45.9**
Add **14.6** and **45.7**

Work the answers out on a separate piece of paper.

31

Adding minus numbers

Numbers with a minus sign in front of them (like this: −5) are called minus numbers.

Weather forecast

One everyday place to find minus numbers is on a thermometer – especially in Alaska, which is one of the world's coldest places. For example, a weather station recorded **−62°C** on 23 January, 1971! A few days later it was **58°C** warmer!

Here is another example. Suppose a weather forecaster said that the temperature overnight could fall to **−5°C**, but that the next day it might be **19°C** warmer. What would the temperature be then?

To find the answer, we have to add **19** to **−5**:

$$(-5) + 19 = ?$$

We can use a thermometer marked off to cover the range of temperatures we are interested in like the one shown on the right. Notice that a thermometer is used like an adding ruler.

$$(-5) + 19 = 14$$

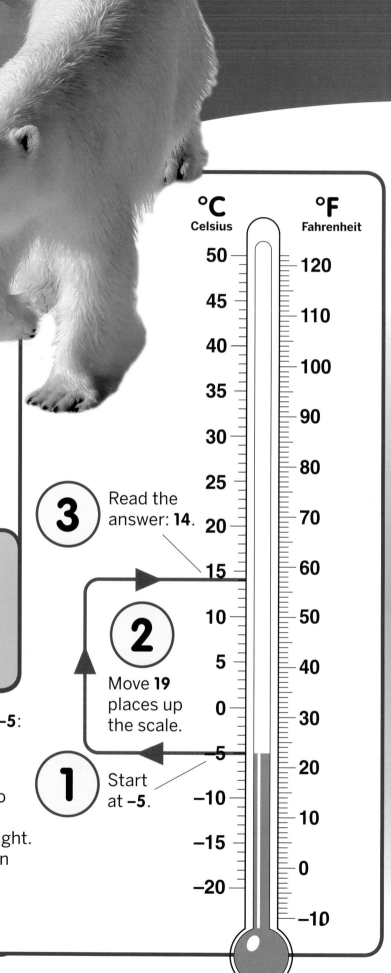

3 Read the answer: **14**.

2 Move **19** places up the scale.

1 Start at **−5**.

Mountains and weather danger

If you go walking in mountains, the day might start out fine and sunny. But the weather changes quickly on a mountain and the wind can get up in no time at all.

Wind makes it feel colder. The stronger the wind, the more quickly heat is taken from your skin and the colder it feels.

Even a slight breeze may make it feel **−5°C** cooler, so a temperature of **9°C** would feel like:

$$9 + (-5) = 4°C$$

But in mountains the temperature might be just **2°C** and the wind might be very strong. If this were the case the wind might make it feel **−20°C** colder and it would feel like:

$$2 + (-20) = -18°C$$

Without suitable warm clothing, you would quickly die in such conditions. Now you can see why the people in this mountain picture are so heavily wrapped up.

Can you do this? Using the information on Alaska on the opposite page, can you say what the temperature was in Alaska after it had risen **58°C**?

Give your answer on a separate piece of paper.

Adding fractions

A fraction is a piece of something.

When an apple is cut in half, we are splitting it into **2** pieces, or two fractions.

If those two pieces are put side by side again, the **2** pieces make up, or add up to, the whole apple once more.

We write each half piece as a fraction like this:

$$\frac{1}{2}$$

and say it as 'one-half'.

Now we know that two halves make a whole:

$$\frac{1}{2} + \frac{1}{2} = 1$$

Notice that each fraction has the same number on the bottom. This means we can combine them:

$$\frac{1}{2} + \frac{1}{2} = \frac{2}{2} = 1$$

When the top and bottom are the same number (such as $\frac{2}{2}$), this makes a whole one.

So the rule is, if you have fractions with the same number at the bottom, you can add the tops of the fractions together.

Parts of a fraction:

The number of parts we have (also called numerator)

$$\frac{3}{4}$$

Dividing line

The number of parts the original was split into (also called denominator)

The number of parts we have (also called numerator)

3/4

Dividing line

The number of parts the original was split into (also called denominator)

Smaller pieces

Sometimes we cut things into smaller pieces, with more of them.

Arun was going to cut a chocolate cake into six equal pieces. Each piece was one sixth of the original cake. We can write this as ⅙.

But some of his friends had already eaten so much jelly and ice cream that they said they had no room left for cake. So Arun stopped cutting when he had done half the cake. Oliver ate one piece, and Arun ate another. What was left over was one half of the original cake and one piece which was one sixth of the original. How much was that altogether?

If Arun had cut it all, the one half (½) he did not cut would have become three sixths (³⁄₆).

Then it is clearer that:

$$\frac{1}{2} + \frac{1}{6} \quad = \frac{3}{6} + \frac{1}{6} \quad = \frac{4}{6}$$

If you look carefully at the picture can you see that the answer, four sixths (⁴⁄₆), is the same amount as two thirds (²⁄₃)?

Can you do these?

¹⁄₅ + ²⁄₅ = ?

¹⁄₅ + ³⁄₅ = ?

¹⁄₅ + ³⁄₁₀ = ?

Work the answers out on a separate piece of paper.

>>> **Remember...** To add fractions, the bottoms must be the same. If they are, just add the tops.

Adding to an equation

An equation puts two things of equal value either side of an equals sign.

The word 'equation' and the word 'equals' both come from the same Latin word meaning level. You can see how this came about by thinking of the way that scales work. This diagram shows a pair of scales. On one side there are **4** cartons, and on the other side there are **2** bags.

So the scales show us the equation:

4 cartons = 2 bags

Let's shorten this to:

4c = 2b

Now, if we add **5** jars (**5j**) to the cartons, the scale pan with the jars and cartons will be heavier than the scale pan with the bags.

4c + 5j ≠ 2b

Is not equal to

To bring the scales back into balance again, you need to add the same amount to both sides, like this:

Now the equation is balanced again:

4c + 5j = 2b + 5j

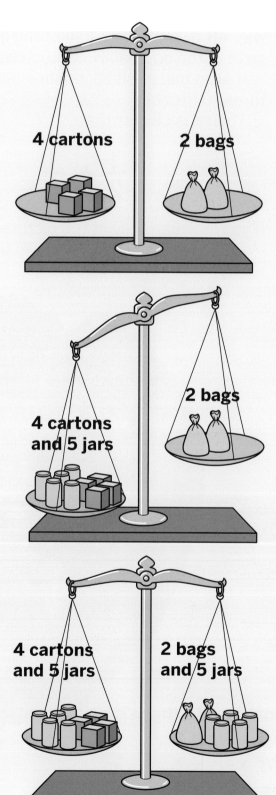

4 cartons   2 bags

4 cartons and 5 jars   2 bags

4 cartons and 5 jars   2 bags and 5 jars

Finding unknowns

Knowing that an equation balances allows us to find an unknown number in questions like:

$$8 + \boxed{?} = 9 + 5$$

Here we need to know which number **?** added to **8** will equal **9 + 5**

From our adding facts we already know that **9 + 5 = 14**

so:

$$8 + \boxed{?} = 14$$

By using our adding facts backwards, we should also know that **8 + 6 = 14**
So the unknown number is **6**:

$$8 + \boxed{?} = 14$$

Notice that using adding facts backwards is something we have not done before, but as you can see, it is very helpful.

Starting with

$$x + 6 = 8 + 7$$

what is **x**?

1   Add the two numbers on the right

$$x + 6 = 15$$

2   Notice that **15 = 9 + 6**
This is handy because if we split up **15** this way, we will have a **6** on both sides of the equation.

$$x + 6 = 9 + 6$$

3   Take away **6** from both sides to give the answer:

$$x = 9$$

 Remember... If we do the same thing to both sides of an equation, it remains balanced.

Can you do this?

Here is an equation: **x + 5 = 8 + 7**   what is **x**?

Give your working out on a separate piece of paper.

Distance charts

If you want to plan a route for your holiday, you need to add distances.

There are many ways of writing down numbers. In atlases it is common to see a distance chart looking like a triangle. To find the distance, you read the first place along the row and the second place up the column.

Distance charts allow you to work out how far your trip will be. But you will need to add each distance together to get the distance of the trip.

Donald and Glenn were planning a journey across Canada with their parents.

They had bought a road map that included a distance chart. They needed to see how far they would travel in total.

Adding the distances

Here are the distances that Donald and Glenn got from the chart on the right.

Vancouver to Calgary **1,090 km**
Calgary to Winnipeg **1,350 km**
Winnipeg to Montreal **2,390 km**
Montreal to Halifax **1,280 km**

Now they had to add them up.
Check to see that you agree with them.

Distance in km

	Halifax	Montreal	Saskatoon	Vancouver	Winnipeg
Calgary	5,011	3,750	626	1,090	1,350
Halifax		1,280	4,448	5,995	3,655
Montreal			3,184	4,731	2,390
Saskatoon				1,681	783
Vancouver					2,330
Winnipeg					

1 Put the numbers below each other in a column, lining them up to the right. Add the right-hand column first. In this case it is:

0 + 0 + 0 + 0 = 0
So write down **0**.

2 Add the next column to the left. This is the tens column. From the bottom up this is:

8 + 9 + 5 + 9 = 31
So write down **1**, carry **3**.

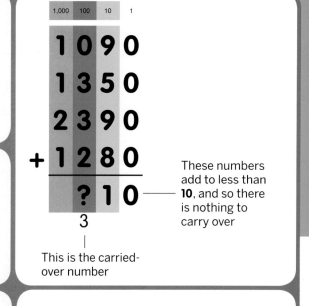

These numbers add to less than **10**, and so there is nothing to carry over

This is the carried-over number

3 Add next column to the left. This is the hundreds column. First add the carried-over **3** to the bottom number:

(3) + 2 + 3 + 3 + 0 = 11
So write down **1** and carry **1** to the next column left.

Add the next column to the left. This is the thousands column. First add the carried-over **1** to the bottom number:

(1) + 1 + 2 + 1 + 1 = 6
So write down **6**.

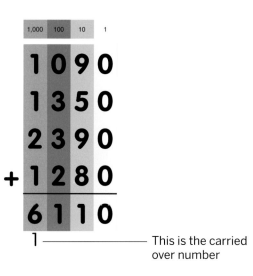

This is the carried over number

4 The total journey was **6,110 km** – a journey of a lifetime!

Remember… **0's** are place holders. Notice that many distances end in **0**. But you cannot ignore the **0** because it is part of the number. It is holding the place of no units. You must add **0's** just like any other number.

Can you do this? Find the distance travelled if they went from Winnipeg to Calgary to Vancouver.

Give your working out on a separate piece of paper.
Then use an atlas to find out if that would have been a sensible journey.

What symbols mean

Here is a list of the common maths symbols together with an example of how they are used.

+ The symbol for adding. We say it 'plus'. In Latin plus means 'more'.

– Between two numbers this symbol means 'subtract' or 'minus'. In front of one number it means the number is a minus number. In Latin minus means 'less'.

= The symbol for equals. We say it 'equals' or 'makes'. It comes from a Latin word meaning 'level' because weighing scales are level when the amounts on each side are equal.

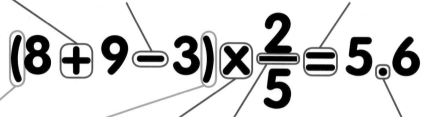

$$(8 + 9 - 3) \times \frac{2}{5} = 5.6$$

( ) The symbols for brackets. You do everything inside the brackets first. Brackets always occur in pairs.

✕ The symbol for multiplying. We say it 'multiplied by' or 'times'.

─, **/** and **÷** Three symbols for dividing. We say it 'divided by'. A pair of numbers above and below a **/** or **─** make a fraction, so $^2/_5$ or $\frac{2}{5}$ is the fraction two-fifths.

. This is a decimal point. It is a dot written after the units when a number contains parts of a unit as well as whole numbers. This is the decimal number five point six.

Index

adding 4, *and throughout*
    decimal numbers 30–31
    fractions 34–35
    large numbers 39
    minus numbers 32–33
    single-digit numbers 4–23
    three-digit numbers 28–29
    two-digit numbers 20–27
    using columns 14–15, 21, 24–31, 39
    using patterns 10–11
    using rulers 6–9

adding facts 12–13, 18–23
adding square 18–19, 22–23
carrying 21, 24–29, 39
counting on 4–5
distance charts 38–39
equals 36–37
equations 36–37
number line 6
place holder 39
place value 2
Turn-Around Rule 16–17, 23